Courageous Women In the Bible

Step Out in Faith

Live Life With Purpose

D0367279

Julie-Allyson Ieron

wesleyan
PUBLISHING HOUSE
wphstore.com

Copyright © 2006 by Wesleyan Publishing House
Published by Wesleyan Publishing House
Indianapolis, Indiana 46250
Printed in the United States of America

ISBN: 978-0-89827-337-3

To the Reader

I write to you as a friend—as a fellow journeyer on the trek toward knowing God in new and intimate ways. Like you, I'm busy. I'm often overwhelmed and frequently weary. I don't need one more assignment to add to my long to-do list that would take well into the second Tuesday of next week to complete. And yet, I have a longing to know God—who He is, what He wants from me, what He has planned for me. As part of that longing, I've been getting to know the many women whose stories appear in His Word. In knowing them—how they came to faith, how they lived their lives, how they interacted with the God of the universe—I have come to understand many new truths about the real purpose God had when He created woman. And I have come to understand something about the real purpose God had when He created you and me.

So, I invite you on this journey of discovery. We'll meet women who had families, women who had a message from God, women who felt the hand of God's Son on their lives. We'll also meet women who faced tragic and trying circumstances, women who made some questionable decisions, and women who found God faithful and true to His word. In short, we'll meet sisters in faith who faced the same struggles we face.

This is a practical journey, one that has a great deal of relevance to the lives we live in this day. So, alongside the stories of Bible women, you'll read brief snippets from women of our millennium—women of faith from all walks of life who are demonstrating what it means to put Bible lessons into practice.

You may choose to take this journey alone or as part of a small group or Bible class. If you take it alone, I challenge you to find a trusted friend who can help you process the decisions you'll make along the way—someone who can help hold you accountable before God for the commitments you'll make to living in a closer and deeper relationship with His Son, Jesus Christ.

If you choose to take this journey as part of a regular group meeting, take some time before going to your meeting to read the brief introductory sections, "For Openers" and "Getting to Know Her," as well as the primary Scripture passage for that week's session.

By taking a few moments out of your week to prepare your heart, you'll find a richer and fuller experience all along the way.

So, come on. Let me introduce you to some amazing sisters, women who touched the heart of God.

To the Leader

I hope you're excited about beginning this journey together. The women of the Bible have so much to teach us as women of the twenty-first century. Their homes and conveniences might have looked different, but their challenges were much like ours. They experienced the stress of raising a family, the frustration of dealing with difficult people and out-of-control circumstances, and the strain of making a living and a home. They also desired to know God and better understand what He wanted to do in their lives.

As the leader, you'll have the great privilege of shepherding group members in their discussions and in their commitments. You'll lead them through the study and guide them toward biblical answers to the circumstances of their lives. It is important that you prepare personally for each session both by reading the text and by praying for God to be present and active during the discussion time.

The body of each week's session contains—

For Openers — a contemporary setting to introduce a key theme from the woman's life and to help provide a modern-day angle on it.

Getting to Know Her — an overview of the main Scripture passage that will help put a real face on the Bible woman.

These first two sections should take about one-fourth of your total session time.

The Word Speaks—a time of reading and interacting with the key Scripture.

Where We Come In—a time of putting ourselves in the scene and making it our own. *Application*

These sections also contain sidebars—

- What Others Say
- Bible Background
- Did You Know?
- How It Works Today

Reading and discussing the questions in "The Word Speaks" and "Where We Come In" sections, along with the sidebar content, will make up the majority of your discussion.

However, just leaving your study at the theoretical stage is insufficient for real life change, so we've included a response section that you'll lead your group through. This is the pivotal moment of the study, where theory and insights translate into right-where-we-live actions. Try to spend about a quarter of your session time on these sections—

Responding through Prayer—where participants approach God and seek His guidance both individually and as a group. Group support is key, as accountability accompanies life change, and group dynamics come together in a special way as we approach God's throne together.

My Next Step—a practical, personal commitment toward life change for each participant.

Keep It in Mind—a simple, brief Bible verse that serves as a reminder throughout the week of the choices made in the session.

Take the first few moments of your time, beginning with your second session together, to ask how each participant applied the previous week's commitments. Encourage the group to feel free to share successes and struggles in this non-judgmental time. Holding one another accountable in this way will urge participants to follow through on the commitments they make each week.

I encourage you to do this shepherding prayerfully and with the grace and compassion that can flow only from your own personal relationship with Jesus Christ. At times the women of your group may need a listening ear, a compassionate challenge, or an act of kindness. At times you may need the same. But mostly you all will need a safe haven where you can learn together from God's Word, try and fail, and get up to try again. May your group become a place where God's presence is felt and where many women come to know Him in new and fresh ways.

When God does amazing things in your group, let us know about these victories. Let us share in the joy of His work in your life.

Contact us by writing to—

Wesleyan Publishing House
P.O. Box 50434
Indianapolis, IN 46250
Attn: Sisters in Faith

Or e-mail us at wph@wesleyan.org.

More Sisters in Faith Bible Studies

Transformed Women in the Bible
Explore Real Life Issues—Experience Real Life Change

Sisters in the Bible
Celebrate Relationships—Experience God's Power

Contents

Introduction

The twenty-first-century, western world doesn't value many traits of its predecessors. Old-time faith it deems a crutch. Willingness to follow it finds distasteful. Selflessness it considers fruitless. And bowing at the throne of anyone other than oneself it regards as deluded.

Yet the postmodern world has aligned at least one of its values with that of previous generations: courage. Raw, unadulterated courage. Watch any action movie or sporting event. Most of our heroes are muscular, superhuman figures that dodge villains, race through pain, and fly down a track at two hundred miles per hour.

But that's not true courage. I'm watching true courage play out before me as I write, sitting at the bedside of my friend Carla in the hospital cancer ward. Serving with grace and compassion, as the nurses and aides are doing—that's courage. Facing a life-threateningillness with faith—that's courage. Remaining hopeful through demeaning tests, invasive exams, and painful procedures—that's courage.

This breed of courage is closer to the supernatural bravery modeled by women of both Old Testament and New Testament fame—women who demonstrated the willingness to follow God's wisdom despite the cost, despite human logic, and despite imminent danger.

I'd like to introduce you in the coming sessions to eight women of extraordinary valor. You'll meet Deborah, who wielded her authority to provide godly wisdom and a military victory to the people of Israel; Abigail and Esther, who audaciously provided wise counsel to kings disposed to act in anger; Huldah the prophetess, who gave God's hard judgment to a godly king; Jehosheba the princess, who risked her own life to save a prince; Anna, who gave her life away in selfless worship; Damaris and Priscilla, who sought and found the truth of Jesus Christ—and then demonstrated the courage to teach it.

These are women you'll come to love—women who will challenge your assumptions, your decisions, and your preconceived notions of true courage.

1

Wisdom For A Nation

Judges 4:3–24

Deborah, a prophetess, the wife of Lappidoth, was leading Israel at that time. She held court under the Palm of Deborah between Ramah and Bethel in the hill country of Ephraim, and the Israelites came to her to have their disputes decided.

—Judges 4:4–5

Discovery

Acting on God's direction requires courage.

For Openers

As a young woman, I was excited when, in 1981, Ronald Reagan nominated Sandra Day O'Connor as the first woman justice of the U.S. Supreme Court. Perhaps you were among the countless women inspired by the justice's example. For twenty-five years her decisions affected the direction and the morality of a nation. While we may or may not agree with all those decisions, we acknowledge the authority of her office and the respect she earned.

We, too, are judges, and this role is played out in various ways in our lives, ranging from refereeing toddler turf-wars to negotiating high-dollar budgets and contracts. Regardless, the act of judging calls for us to listen intently to both sides of the argument, consider incomplete evidence, discern between truth and deception, and courageously act.

Only the Judge of the Universe has the authority to pass ultimate judgment. But that Judge temporarily delegates some of that authority to His children, to use with wisdom and fairness for the betterment of His people in this world. Deborah, whom we'll meet today, was a woman given this special authority.

Getting to Know Her

The setting is bleak: Israel is caught in a cycle in which the people of God keep forgetting every miraculous way God has delivered them out of bondage and into the lush land of promise. They keep serving other gods, making vile sacrifices to idols, and getting into heaps of trouble. Then they call out to Yahweh, and He raises up a judge who leads them to victory over their enemies. When the judge dies, the people go back to their sinful ways — until they are again sinking in quagmire.

This cycle has already taken place three times when we meet Deborah: a woman, a prophetess (that is, a spokesperson for God), and a judge over civil disputes. Jack Hayford calls her "the first female Supreme Court Justice." Her story is one of courage, discernment, and decisive action at God's direction.

Her courtroom is quite a sight: a huge palm tree, fronds swaying with every breath of wind, providing respite from midday heat and shelter from the elements. Throngs of plaintiffs and accusers create a stir. In the midst of it all sits a regal woman—motherly, compassionate, and other-worldly wise.

In a culture where women are traditionally subservient, Judge [*unusual*] Deborah is trusted enough that all abide by her decisions. She wields authority that could only come from heaven. Like the two judges before her, she receives God's direction to do battle against the people's oppressors. So Israel's troops and its two leaders (one spiritual and one military) go out to meet Sisera and his army of chariots. God sends a heavy rain to make the battlefield a muddy quagmire and gives His people a decisive victory (see Judges 5:20–21). Immediately, Deborah and Barak compose a song of praise to God and sing it before the people of Israel.

The Word Speaks

Have someone from the group read aloud **Judges 4:3-24**.

The text describes Deborah as the people's judicial voice, a prophetess who listens to God's word and speaks it with boldness. But, unlike anyone else in Scripture, she is described as "a mother in Israel" (Judges 5:7). Why might God place a woman—a mother—in this role at this moment in His people's history?

Knew Barak was not up to it.

When and why did the people finally cry out to God? Why do you suppose it took such dire circumstances?

When Sisera was coming to destroy them.
He had 900 Iron Chariots - Israelites had none
They were not feeling the danger

Put yourself under the Palm of Deborah. When the word of God comes to her and directs her to send ten thousand men into a war that seems impossible to win, what fears might she face? What emotions might she experience?

What Others Say

When God answers a prayer, it is not the final closing curtain on an episode in our lives. Rather, it is the opening of the curtain to the next act. The most important part of prayer is what we do with God's answers . . . He expects us to be prepared to act or to be acted upon by His answer to our prayers.

—Evelyn Christensen

Read the quote from Evelyn Christensen and comment on what God expects the people and their leaders (Deborah and Barak) to do as part of His answer to their prayers. Why does God call for their obedience and participation in their deliverance?

Read the quote from Oswald Chambers. Have you ever upset someone else's plans by following God's leading? What did Deborah's obedience cost the enemy? Her own troops? What did Barak's unwillingness to go to battle without Deborah cost him? Why?

What Others Say

If we are in love with our Lord, obedience does not cost us anything, it is a delight, but it costs those who do not love Him a good deal. If we obey God it will mean that other people's plans are upset.

—Oswald Chambers

If courage is a quality that allows a person to face danger with bravery and confidence, what elements of the story indicate that Deborah is a courageous woman?

Needs - Obeys God's Command

Consider two common words we derive from courage: encourage and discourage. Which characters in this story practice encouragement? Which characters practice discouragement? (Consider the supporting cast, as well.)

Deborah - encourage

Barak - discourage

The battle between Sisera and Israel was fought in the place we now call Megiddo. This is where the book of Revelation says the King of Kings will win His final, decisive victory—the battle we commonly refer to as Armageddon. How does this detail change your perspective on the significance of this victory accomplished supernaturally by God? Comment on the symbolism for the future battle.

Sisera - thought he had victory - God intervenes
Armageddon - won't have victory   "   "

Where We Come In

Read the quote from Jack Hayford. Are you willing to allow God's Spirit to develop your capacities to shape the world around you? What qualities or gifts of yours do you think God could use in this way? Does this excite or frighten you?

Did You Know?

Deborah literally means "Bee," reminding us of this woman's wisdom, how she liberally shared with her friends, and how her influence and authority were used by God to "sting" Israel's enemies. Her creative talents and leadership abilities distinguish her.

—Jack Hayford

When you're in a seemingly impossible situation, as Deborah was, where do you turn? What or who bolsters your courage and gives you strength to move forward?

 Turn to Joshua 1:1–9. Note and discuss the similarities between God's encouragement to Joshua and His word through Deborah to General Barak.

Read Michelle's story. How does her courageous dependence on God challenge you? Describe a situation that called you to exhibit courage. How did you keep from becoming discouraged? Did you experience God's prompting? How did you know it was His voice? How did His presence make you feel and act differently than you would have if you had felt alone in the situation?

How It Works Today

Michelle Strombeck is a producer for the Christian radio station WMBI. In her thirties, single and energetic, she leads an ordered life with just the right level of excitement. But over Christmas 2004, as she watched reports of the Indian Ocean Tsunami, she was filled with grief.

Michelle felt God's tugging to do more than send money, so she volunteered to join a relief team. Less than two weeks later, Michelle flew to the affected region to distribute aid. But her team was threatened bodily by a rebel faction of the Indonesian army. She describes her response as abject fear for her life. Some of the team wanted to quit. But God gave Michelle the courage to fulfill her promise and distribute the aid—practical items like woks, plates and cooking utensils, blankets, sarongs, cooking oil, and wash tubs. Like a tenderhearted mother, she listened to the people's stories, wept with them, and silently represented Christ.

Read Judges 2:16–19, then make a list of the ways the Israelites consistently failed God. Now, go through that list and compare it to similar costly choices you have recently made. Be as candid and specific as you can.

4. In Hebrews 13:5–6 God promises: "'Never will I leave you; never will I forsake you.' So we say with confidence, 'The Lord is my helper; I will not be afraid.'" This sounds similar to the promise He made to Joshua and to the way He continually came to the rescue of His people. How does reading this promise make you feel? What does it give you the courage to accomplish?

God's compassion for His wandering children is a constant in His character. Consider the following promise: "If we are faithless, he will remain faithful, for he cannot disown himself" (2 Tim. 2:13). How does it encourage you to know that even when you sin, you can run home to God, confess your sins, and receive forgiveness and the blessing of His voice leading you back?

Bible Background

Deborah herself wasn't the emphasis. Her usefulness to God and to the nation of Israel was what mattered . . . Even after the victory over Sisera, when it would have been tempting to take some personal credit, Deborah sang a song in praise of the Lord.

—June Gunden

Read the quote from June Gunden. What difference does it make who gets the credit in this story? Who gets the credit for victories in your life? Who should get the credit? In what specific ways can you begin to give credit—praise, thanks, or adoration—where it is due?

Talk about Jael

19

Like Deborah, express your gratitude aloud to God who offers you deliverance, just as He offered His people many years ago.

Responding through Prayer

Make this your heart's prayer: *God, as much as I'd like to say I'm always like Deborah, I know that sometimes I am more like the Israelites who kept sinning against You. I'm thinking of when I disobeyed You by* _____. *Forgive me for this sin. Give me the strength to be courageous this week. Thank You for Your faithfulness to me.*

My Next Step

This week I need courage as I face:

Keep It in Mind

Read this Scripture daily as a challenge to yourself: "Be strong and courageous. Do not be terrified; do not be discouraged, for the LORD your God will be with you wherever you go" (Josh. 1:9).

2

Swift, Gracious Action Saves the Day

1 Samuel 25:14–35

Abigail to David: "Let no wrongdoing be found in you as long as you live."
David to Abigail: "May you be blessed for your good judgment."
—1 Samuel 25:28, 33

Discovery

Speaking with conviction makes courage shine.

For Openers

Try to maneuver your car through rush-hour traffic in any city, and you'll know that manners and politeness are diminishing. Watch as commuters zip between clogged lanes, trying desperately to get in front of someone, anyone—*you* especially. Learn to read lips—or hand gestures—and you'll see that mean and surly human traits are far from extinction. It's gotten so bad that a TV newsmagazine recently did an hour-long show titled "What Ever Happened to Manners?"

Most of us have been subject to someone who is mean and surly. A boss, perhaps. Or a disgruntled grocery clerk. Or a DMV agent who clearly doesn't belong in a *service* profession. I'm ashamed to admit that my greatest temptation is to respond to these folks by becoming meaner and surlier in their faces. Sound familiar? Perhaps you've found, as I have, that this tends only to escalate the situation—not the greatest outcome.

The woman we'll meet today was subject to a mean, surly husband. Yet her legacy isn't one of becoming in-his-face surly. Quite the opposite. Her grace, courage, and decisive action skillfully diffused a life-threatening situation for her entire household—surly husband included.

Getting to Know Her

whose father is joy

It's a newsworthy time. Abigail, wife of wealthy sheep owner Nabal, has heard about the death of the godly judge, Samuel; her country has come through a period of mourning for him. King Saul is wielding power unchecked and is seeking the life of the Samuel-anointed king, David. Closer to home, beautiful Abigail is subject to a violent husband, who never fails to live up to his name, which means *fool*.

man of Belial - worthless person

As she goes about her business, Abigail is unaware that her world is about to shift into adrenaline-rush mode. Then, a servant sprints up, so agitated he can hardly get the words out: David has been living in the desert near Nabal's flocks, protecting them from harm without pay. Now, David has asked Nabal for a little food and water—a request Nabal has categorically denied. What's worse, he's insulted David to his face. Now, David is planning to level Nabal's household.

Without a moment to waste, Abigail gathers a huge care package—far more than hospitality would require. These provisions she takes from the best of her household's store, loads them on donkeys, and sends her servants to David. She follows the procession on her donkey—resolute despite her pounding heart. Riding into the mountain ravine where David is fuming and assembling troops, she dismounts, genuflects, and apologizes so profusely, so skillfully, so soothingly, that *flatters* David's anger evaporates. Tactfully, she counsels him not to commit *praises* the sin of murder, but to leave justice in the Almighty's hands.

Nabal → dies - Struck down by God

David acquiesces and thanks her for saving him from bloodshed. He takes notice of this woman whose wisdom and humility do him a great service of good. And that's where the story gets really hot.

The Word Speaks

As you read **1 Samuel 25:14-35** aloud, have four volunteers serve as dramatic readers; have one be Nabal's servant; one Abigail; one David; and one the narrator.

Read the note from *Nelson's New Illustrated Bible Commentary*. How does this cultural detail help you to understand why David would be so angered by Nabal's refusal to fulfill his request?

Did You Know?

Nabal lived in a wilderness area and owned thousands of sheep and goats, and so was a prime target for thieves. David and his men had generously protected Nabal's flocks and possessions (vv. 15, 16, 21). Since it was the time of sheepshearing, Nabal would have had plenty of cash from the sale of wool to reward David and his men for their services.

—*Nelson's New Illustrated Bible Commentary*

Why is it significant that the servant rushes to Abigail? What risk is he taking in bypassing his master's wishes?

He doesn't want to be killed by David's men

Picture Abigail, first hurrying to assemble the generous provisions, then bouncing across the countryside on her donkey. What dangers is she taking on by acting quickly? What might she be thinking as she rides?

Will David listen to her - could kill her
What will Nabal think & do to her.

How do the traits of tact, humility, and honesty play out in her diplomatic exchange with David? How do decisive actions combine with persuasive words to affect David's decision?

How is Abigail's faith evident? (Pay special attention to verses 28–31.) What does her insight say about her awareness of events in her country—without the benefit of CNN or *The New York Times*?

Bible Background

Abigail was a wise reprover of David's passion, and he gave an obedient ear to the reproof, according to his own principle (Ps. 141:5): "Let the righteous smite me, it shall be a kindness." Never was such an admonition either better given or better taken.

—Matthew Henry, quoting KJV

Read the quote from Matthew Henry, and then read Psalm 141:5. Discuss the integrity of David, as he not only talks about receiving righteous rebuke but also graciously accepts it from a woman.

Scan 1 Samuel 25:36–42. Why do you suppose Abigail waits to tell Nabal what she has done? Why is it necessary for her to tell him at all? How is God's vengeance on Nabal more righteous than David's would have been?

What is it about the new widow Abigail that so captivates David *wisdom beauty* that he wants to take her as his wife? What does Abigail give up to become a member of David's harem? (Remember: David is to *become* king, but he now lives in a desert encampment. She has been the mistress of a wealthy household.) What does her humility in accepting the proposal that comes through David's men add to your understanding of Abigail's character?

She knows David is Man of God

Where We Come In

What surly or mean individuals have you been subject to? How have their cruel actions had a negative impact on you—whether they physically endangered you or bruised your spirit? What questions do these powerful individuals raise in your heart? Pause to express those questions to God as a group, and ask Him to work good from these situations—just like He did for Abigail and David.

What Others Say

Seize each opportunity, knowing that it may be the last. For it is certainly true that no situation presents itself twice the same. The opportunities of today are not those of tomorrow. Do not live as though they might be repeated. Do not fail to enter every open door.

—Frances J. Roberts

Consider how quickly and decisively Abigail acted, then read the quote from Frances Roberts. What situations have you encountered that called for immediate action? What situations have called for wise words to diffuse anger? How has God equipped you to handle these issues?

What is the difference between Abigail's quick action, and David's intention to act rashly? In a crisis, how can we tell the difference between the two? What patterns does Abigail's example provide that will help you the next time circumstances call you to act wisely and quickly?

Note how Abigail speaks well—and rightly—of the Lord's promises (25:30). What reminders do you need of the Lord's promises to you—and of His provision for you? Why is this portion of her speech convicting to David? To you?

Read the story of Karen Smith and the way her ministry gifts bless both her husband and her church. How is she like a modern-day Abigail in her support and encouragement of her godly husband? If you know a woman like her, tell the group about that woman's example to you.

How It Works Today

Karen Smith is the first lady of a church of several thousand in Arlington Heights, Illinois. Her husband, Colin, became senior pastor there a decade ago, after sixteen years of pastoring in London. (Karen was born in England; Colin in Scotland.)

The couple (and their sons, then ages eight and ten) began getting to know people in their congregation by inviting small groups of members into their home. After a few months, they had hosted every member. They count as their nearest friends many of those they hosted. Karen now serves the church by visiting shut-in and hospitalized members, who are comforted by her genuine smile.

But her service doesn't end with hospitality. She listens to her husband preview his sermons and occasionally suggests a word or title. Recently, when Colin preached a series on marriage, he quipped that Karen had "approved and sanctioned" his message. She laughed. But at the close of the service, she joined him at the microphone and prayed on behalf of all the congregation's wives. Her words and her actions show how grateful she is that Colin is using his gifts (and she, hers) for God's kingdom.

What Others Say

When we, confused by negative thinking, are in danger of making a wrong decision, may we also meet someone who warns us, who shows us the right way, who has our good conscience at heart. That is a gift of peace from God.

—Gien Karssen

Read the quote from Gien Karssen. Tell the group about a mentor or friend who has helped you avert a bad decision. How was this person a "gift of peace from God" to you? Did you feel that way immediately, or did it take you some time to recognize the voice of God in that person's words?

How can you bring to life some of the traits of Abigail in your household? In your workplace? In your church?

Responding through Prayer

As you pray, begin by thanking God for a specific person who has been a wise counselor to you. Continue by claiming a promise from His Word to you. Finish by asking God to make you a humble yet persuasive servant like Abigail. Be brief enough to allow time for every member to speak a sentence prayer on each subject.

My Next Step

I will contact a friend who is sad or troubled, and I will encourage her with promises from God's Word, with prayer, and with the following tangible provisions that can help sustain her through her desert experience:

Keep It in Mind

While it can be overwhelming to try to be like the Proverbs 31 woman, apply this piece of wisdom from her life to your conduct this week: "She speaks with wisdom, and faithful instruction is on her tongue" (Prov. 31:26).

3

The Power
Of One

2 Kings 11:1–8, 17–21

*One thing I ask of the LORD, this is what I seek: that
I may dwell in the house of the LORD . . . For in the day
of trouble he will keep me safe in his dwelling.*

—Psalm 27:4, 5

Discovery

One courageous woman can change the world.

For Openers

The airwaves are clogged with newsmakers and talk show participants who are quick to deny personal blame for their actions. The murderer was acting at his gang's direction; the thief stole because her addiction made her; the drug dealer should be excused because he grew up without a father figure. However, before we can wag a finger at these dodgers, our own cowardice to accept responsibility rears up to accuse us.

Courage takes many shapes. Sometimes, as in the case of the military and judicial leader Deborah, it calls for authoritative action— with the joyous participation of those who most need the intervention. In other cases, courage calls for action that is contrary to one's upbringing, one's peers, and the human propensity to pass the blame.

If anyone had reason to plead a dysfunctional background, it was the woman we'll meet today. Her family history would put to shame any self-respecting soap opera family of the twenty-first century. Yet she made a courageous choice—at risk of her life— that still speaks volumes about the rewards of breaking free from the chains that bind us.

Getting to Know Her

A week before Christmas, our pastor listed his sermon title as "The Woman Who Saved Christmas." The buzz around the sanctuary was full of guesses about who this woman might be. Most expected Mary to be the one. But they were way off—not even in the right generation. More than a few Bible quizzers have been stumped by this woman's name: Jehosheba. While she isn't mentioned in the long lineage of Jesus (as are Bathsheba and Ruth), she did play an integral part in the Christmas story.

It all starts when God makes good on His promise to His prophet Elijah (1 Kings 19:16–17) that He will cut off the descendants of the wicked King Ahab of Israel. The only problem is, the kingdom of Judah is ruled by Ahab's grandson, Ahaziah—an evil king, in the tradition of his mother, Athaliah, and his grandmother, Jezebel. In a grizzly scene, Ahaziah and his cousins—all Ahab's line—are murdered.

Queen Athaliah immediately seizes Judah's throne, demanding that all the rightful heirs, her grandsons, be slaughtered. This would finish the job of cutting off the royal line of David, from which the Messiah is supposed to descend.

This travesty doesn't take the Almighty by surprise, though. Years before, He'd arranged the unlikely marriage of Jehosheba, Ahaziah's half-sister, to Jehoiada, the high priest who served faithfully in His Temple. So, at just the right moment and at great danger, Jehosheba sneaks into the palace, amid the chaos, and rescues her brother's youngest heir, one-year-old Joash. She and Jehoiada hide the child in a secret room of Solomon's temple for six years. Thus the royal line—and Christmas—is saved.

The Word Speaks

Have someone read aloud **2 Kings 11:1-8, 17-21**.

This story is also told in a parallel passage in 2 Chronicles. There we learn Jehoram, father of Ahaziah and Jehosheba, was so evil that "He passed away, to no one's regret, and was buried in the City of David, but not in the tombs of the kings" (2 Chron. 21:20). How does this help you understand the upbringing of these two siblings?

Why wasn't this background an excuse for Ahaziah to continue his father's evil ways? How did God hold both men accountable?

Read the quote from Matthew Henry. Comment on the fact that although Jehoram was evil, he was useful to God's plan of saving the royal line.

What world events or historical events have demonstrated that God will move His purposes forward, despite evil powers? How do these stories encourage you?

In a few matter-of-fact verses, we learn of the courage of a princess, all but exiled to life as the wife of an elderly priest in the Temple. (Jehoiada may have been around eighty years old; Jehosheba was most likely in her early twenties.) What motivated Jehosheba to risk her life for her infant nephew? What influence might her husband have had on her? How can a young woman with a horrendous background come by such courage?

Put yourself in the place of the few godly people left in Judah as they endured the six-year reign of Athaliah. Discuss their desperation, disappointment, and fear. Then discuss the range of emotions of Jehosheba, Jehoiada, and the child's nurse—the only people who knew for sure that God still had a plan.

Read 2 Samuel 7:12–16 to learn of God's promise of the Messiah to come through David's royal line. Then read the note from *Bible Reader's Companion*. Is this promise ever really in jeopardy—despite the well-laid plans of Satan? Why not?

Bible Background

In a statement that echoes throughout all time [2 Sam. 7:16], God promises to maintain David's house/line forever. . . . This great promise, the Davidic Covenant, is echoed by the prophets, and is fulfilled in Jesus Christ, David's Descendant and Lord of an eternal kingdom. In response, all David can do is fall on his knees and praise God.

—Bible Reader's Companion

What is the significance of the fact that David's last descendant found shelter and safety in the house of the Lord? Consider Psalm 27:4–5 and other facts you can recall about David's love for God's house and his dream to build a temple.

Where We Come In

Read 2 Chronicles 24:17–19. The sad part of this story is that after such godly influence and training, King Joash only served God as long as Jehoiada lived. After the priest's death, Joash trusted evil advisers and was gravely displeasing to God; he died in disgrace (2 Chron. 24:25). How does this end of a formerly God-influenced man provide a warning to you? What influence do the friends surrounding you have on the choices you make?

Read the story about peer pressure in How It Works Today. What temptations do you face because of your friends, mentors, and counselors? How have you made decisions about whom to trust? After whom do you pattern your life? What do you intend to do differently after reading of the dangers of being influenced by the wrong people?

When you've been in danger or in distress, how have you found comfort in God's presence and among His people?

How It Works Today

I was a chubby, freckle-faced child, a model student, and class punching bag—definitely not "in-crowd" material.

At a new school in seventh grade, I was determined to fit in—to become more like my peers. A Bible-study friend of my mother's had a daughter in my homeroom. She sponsored my entrance into the in-crowd, introduced me at the lunchroom *in* table, and invited me to her in-girl sleepover. I figured we'd spend the night talking about boys and doing each other's hair. But instead, the girls decided to hold a séance. The spirit about the place suddenly made me shiver. I knew it would grieve Jesus if I participated. So, I crawled into my sleeping bag, put my pillow over my head, and spent the night praying silently.

The next Monday the in-girls still wanted to be friends, but I had changed. I returned to the *out* lunch table—not because I had to, but because I wanted to. Several at that table were handicapped, in wheelchairs, or in remedial classes. These friends may not have worn the right clothes or had the right connections, but with them I didn't have to cover my faith with a sleeping bag and a pillow.

Read the note from *Nelson's New Illustrated Bible Dictionary*. Knowing that <u>Jehosheba</u> means "Jehovah-<u>sworn</u>" or "<u>Yahweh is an oath</u>," discuss how Jehosheba lived up to her name. How did God prove himself faithful to her—as she acted in His will? How was Jehosheba's name a testimony to the oath God had made to her forefather? How has God proven himself faithful to you?

> **Did You Know?**
>
> The naming of a baby was very important in the Bible. In choosing a name, the parents could reflect the circumstances of the child's birth, their own feelings, their gratitude to God, their hopes and prayers for the child, and their commitment of the child to God.
>
> —*Nelson's New Illustrated Bible Dictionary*

When has God made it clear to you that you were to take an action requiring courage? How did you know God was leading you? How did you respond?

Of all the character traits of God, one of the most comforting may be the fact that His word is to be trusted; what He says, He does. How does being certain of God's word give you courage to act in faith, against the odds of those things or people who would keep you from doing right?

We see today that Jehosheba was certainly courageous + obedient to God.

Responding through Prayer

Is there something God is asking you to do now (or soon) that will require a step of faith? Share this with the group, and ask them to pray for you—that you'll have the courage to act and that the hand of God will bless your efforts.

My Next Step

This week I will:

- Reevaluate the following relationships that influence the choices I make.

- Strengthen those that are beneficial and weaken my bonds with those that influence me to make bad decisions.

-

Keep It in Mind

Let this wise counsel guide you this week: "Do not associate with one easily angered, for you may learn his ways and get yourself ensnared" (Prov. 22:24b–25).

4

When The Truth Hurts

2 Kings 22:11–20

*Tell the king of Judah, who sent you to inquire of the LORD,
"This is what the LORD, the God of Israel, says concerning
the words you heard: Because your heart was responsive
and you humbled yourself before the LORD . . .
I have heard you declares the LORD."*

—2 Kings 22:18–19

Discovery

Courage sets you apart from the crowd.

For Openers

I caught myself saying it the other day. As I heard the words come out of my mouth, my heart sank. I had succumbed. Perhaps this week, you've succumbed, too. What is the grievous phrase? Probably not what you're thinking. It isn't a bad word. It isn't mean or vindictive. Not even a juicy bit of gossip. It is the preface, "Well, to tell you the truth . . ."

Why do I bristle at this phrase? Because it suggests that everything else you're hearing from others — or even from me — isn't the truth. That is tragic. Even Jesus had to use a similar phrase to distinguish His truth from the lies the crowds were hearing elsewhere. The Apostle John quotes Him twenty-five times as prefacing statements with "I tell you the truth . . ."

The woman in today's study lived such a life before Jerusalem's ruling class, that when the time came to seek out a trustworthy word, the king sent messengers to her. She didn't have to preface her hard message with an assurance of truthfulness. Both speaker and hearer knew to anticipate nothing but truth from her mouth.

Getting to Know Her

It has been a few generations since Judah enjoyed a godly king. But then Josiah takes the throne and does right in God's sight. It is a refreshing time for God's faithful prophets and priests. But some things still aren't right: Places of pagan worship still dot the landscape. Prostitutes defile the land. The people continue the detestable practice of sacrificing children to Molech.

Eighteen years into his reign, Josiah decides to refurbish the Lord's Temple, so he sends his trusted advisor, Shaphan, to recruit and pay workers to undertake the repairs. While Shaphan is at the Temple, the high priest, Hilkiah, hands him the Book of the Law recently located amid dust and cobwebs. (Commentators believe this was the book of Deuteronomy.) As Shaphan reads this book to Josiah, the king is terrified. As he learns of the Lord's fury against the people and the consequences of their disobedience, the king shreds his robes in mourning.

Josiah sends Hilkiah, Shaphan, and three other counselors to inquire of the Lord. The men determine to go to the second district of Jerusalem to hear God's word through the prophetess Huldah, whose husband is keeper of the king's wardrobe.

Huldah, prophetess and wife, is going about everyday life when this high-ranking delegation knocks at her door. And the Lord gives her a prophecy. Her heart pounds as she understands the difficult message she must convey. Yet she speaks the truth with authority: the people will suffer all the curses found in Deuteronomy because they have performed all the abominable deeds warned against them. But the Lord gives her a special message for softhearted Josiah. Because he has humbled himself and repented, Josiah will not live to see the devastation.

The Word Speaks

As you read **2 Kings 22:11-20**, have one volunteer be the narrator and voice the words of Josiah; have a second volunteer authoritatively read Huldah's prophecy.

Why do you suppose Josiah decided to freshen up the Temple? Speculate on how God might have been preparing the king's heart for Huldah's message—even then. Comment on God's timing in presenting Deuteronomy to a soft-hearted king at that particular moment.

Take time to read as much of the book of Deuteronomy as you are able. For starters, read 4:25–27 and scan 28:14–68. Imagine yourself in Josiah's place—hearing these words for the first time. Discuss Josiah's response and what it reveals about his character.

Read W. A. Criswell's quote. Other prophets who spoke for God in this era included Jeremiah (possibly the son of Hilkiah the priest [Jer. 1:1] and nephew of Huldah [Jer. 32:7]), Nahum, Zephaniah, and Habbakuk. Speculate on why the royal delegation sought God's word from Huldah rather than one of these prophets. How does someone develop the kind of reputation Huldah must have had for royalty to take notice? What is your reputation? Are you considered trustworthy?

In 2 Samuel 1, good King David was tough on a messenger who brought him bad news (he had the messenger killed). Huldah definitely had disappointing news to report to another good king. What risks was she taking by speaking God's word? What fears would you have if you were in her place?

As you review Huldah's words in 2 Kings 22, what stands out to you? Compare verses 15 and 18. How did God's word to Josiah differ when addressing him as leader of a rebellious people and then as a penitent servant? What do you make of this difference?

Read Matthew Henry's comments on the tone of the message that God spoke through Huldah. What does this tell you about God's ultimate authority? What does it tell you about His delegated authority to men and women who serve under Him?

Bible Background

Huldah returned [Josiah's inquiry] not in the language of a courtier—"Pray give my humble service to his Majesty, and let him know that this is the message I have for him from the God of Israel"; but in the dialect of a prophetess, speaking from him before whom all stand upon the same level—"Tell the man that sent you to me."

—Matthew Henry

Scan 2 Kings 23 to see how the king responded. What do his actions confirm about his character? How are his words and his actions consistent? Read 2 Kings 23:25 for a clue.

Where We Come In

This story describes Huldah's "fifteen minutes of fame." What enabled Huldah to speak with authority? How was her courage a matter of entrusting herself to the God she had spent a lifetime serving in obscurity?

How can you learn to recognize God's voice and to know His Word so clearly that you are equipped to speak it when given the opportunity?

How It Works Today

When Anne Graham Lotz, daughter of evangelist Billy Graham, was a young wife and mother, she felt a "desperate need" to know the Bible. She sought a Bible study group, but couldn't find anyone willing to teach it. Reluctantly, she began to facilitate a group that soon grew to 500 women and spawned nine groups of similar size.

Eventually, Anne began holding "Just Give Me Jesus" conferences, which continue to pack out arenas with women feeling the same desperate need to know God intimately. Those attending (thousands strong in every city) are at once challenged, refreshed, renewed, and reinvigorated in service for Jesus Christ. They learn to read God's Word with new understanding and to fall in love with Jesus, Who already loves them with an everlasting love.

Although she initially was reticent (and says she still gets butterflies when she stands to speak), Anne's ministry bloomed into something great. How amazing that it began with one woman's hunger to learn what God had to say!

Read the story about Bible teacher Anne Graham Lotz. How can you follow her example of becoming a student of God's Word? Why do you suppose Anne places so much faith in the person of Jesus? What does the phrase "Just give me Jesus" mean to you? Discuss how we can convince the world (and ourselves) that Jesus is enough to meet our needs.

What Others Say

Read Tim Hansel's quote. How does "goose-bump courage" apply to Huldah's experience? When have you needed "goose-bump courage"? When have

The Bible is a first-hand story of goose-bump courage in very ordinary people who were invaded by the living God.

—Tim Hansel

you felt like an ordinary servant of God, called upon to speak or act on His behalf? What temptations did you face as you decided whether to obey? What did you decide to do or say?

Read the quote from Adam Clarke. What does it mean if someone possesses "the life of God in her soul"? How can we possess the life of God in our souls? What difference does His power and His authority make in your words, actions, and choices?

What does God's stamp of approval on Huldah (by entrusting her with His message) say to you? Why is it crucial that the message she speaks is soon confirmed by events?

What Others Say

The secret of the Lord was neither with Hilkiah the high priest, Shaphan the scribe, nor any other of the servants of the king, or ministers of the temple! We find from this . . . that a simple woman, possessing the life of God in her soul, may have more knowledge of the Divine testimonies than many of those whose office it is to explain and enforce them.

—Adam Clarke

Consider the power of a life's example. Who might be observing the way you live, speak, and act? What does your life preach about God? Would a watching world (or workplace or family) know the truth of God's love, grace, righteousness, forgiveness, and holiness by observing you? When it comes time for you to speak, will your example make them more or less willing to listen to God's truth? What are some ways you can improve in this area?

Responding through Prayer

Make this your heart's prayer: *God, sometimes I feel like I'm toiling in obscurity—like my daily life isn't valuable to You. Thank You for Huldah's example of faithfulness in the dailiness of life and her usefulness to You. Equip me to learn to recognize Your voice, so that when You call upon me to speak Your truth, I am ready, willing, and able.*

My Next Step

Following Huldah's example, I will take special care beginning today to be sure my words, thoughts, and actions enhance Christ's reputation. I will seek God's help as I do this, particularly when I encounter:

Keep It in Mind

This week, practice this principle from Ephesians 4:29: "Do not let any unwholesome talk come out of your mouths, but only what is helpful for building others up according to their needs, that it may benefit those who listen."

5

The Right Woman At The Right Time

The Book of Esther

Go, gather together all the Jews who are in Susa, and fast for me. . . . I and my maids will fast as you do. When this is done, I will go to the king, even though it is against the law. And if I perish, I perish.

—Esther 4:16

Discovery

God gives us courage to walk into the unknown.

For Openers

The question of how a good God could allow bad things to happen is one that keeps many from trusting Christ. Few of us haven't wrestled with this issue at one time or another. I came face-to-face with it the moment I came face-to-barrel with a robber's gun in my office parking lot several years ago. I was employed by a Christian ministry, yet God allowed three thugs to mug me while I was about His business. My material losses paled in comparison to the emotional loss of security (I still have panic attacks when alone in a parking lot). I recall how callous and harsh the pat answer of God working everything for good sounded—not to mention out of touch with reality.

After the incident, I dissected the scene a million ways. If you've had a similar experience, you've probably done the same. Eventually, I realized that I know God; I've seen Him intervene in my life many times. Although I didn't see Him intervene in this situation, I know Him to be good, loving, and gracious. I don't understand why He sometimes allows evil a temporary victory. But I do know that I serve a good God who, as we'll see today, is working behind the scenes, whether we recognize His hand or fail to acknowledge Him at all.

Getting to Know Her

Hadassah has experienced more than her share of loss and disappointment: orphaned, adopted by her cousin Mordecai, renamed Esther to hide her identity as a member of God's people living in a pagan society.

King Xerxes, angered with Queen Vashti, plans a search for beautiful young women to replenish his harem and to compete to replace Vashti as queen. Esther is taken to the harem to join the competition (whether willingly or unwillingly, we don't know). Her grace and inner beauty distinguish her from the gaggle of giggling girls who have come from elsewhere in the kingdom. The eunuch who runs the harem is so taken with Esther that he gives her the primary apartment, the best beauty products, personal attendants, and gourmet food. All the while, Esther keeps her nationality secret, as her adopted father has asked.

After a year of treatments, it is time for Esther to meet King Xerxes. Her beauty and strength please him so much that he stops the competition and names her queen. Life seems good for Queen Esther.

But then, due to a grudge against Mordecai, the king's primary advisor, Haman, convinces Xerxes to agree to exterminate the Jewish population. The comfortable Esther is thrust into a dilemma: to keep silent will result in the death of her countrymen, but to speak up will almost certainly lead to her own doom.

The Word Speaks
Read **Esther 2:8-18**.

The seventy-year captivity of Judah's people had ended, and a remnant obeyed Jeremiah's prophecy (Jer. 29:10) and returned to the Promised Land (Ezra 1). More than thirty years later, though, most Jews continued to live on pagan soil. Where should the Jews have been, according to God's promises? Why do you suppose so many failed to comply? How does this color your understanding of Esther's story?

What character traits caused Esther to rise to prominence in the harem? (See verses 9 and 15.) How do you suppose a young girl who had been through such loss grew into such a gracious woman? How was she a reflection of her cousin Mordecai? Of God?

Bible Background

The Hebrew word for favor is a term used regularly in the Bible to describe the character of God. This word may be translated "loyal love." The frequency of this concept with regard to Esther in this book may be a subtle way of suggesting the presence of the Lord without actually mentioning His name.

—*The Nelson Study Bible*

Read the note from the *The Nelson Study Bible*. How does this definition of *favor* help define Esther's character?

Now read **Esther 4:11-16** and **5:5-6**.

Earlier Esther needed to exhibit grace; in this part of the story she needed steely resolve, supernatural wisdom, and unadulterated bravery. Where does she find these character traits? When have you needed these traits? How have you found them?

Read the note about fasting. How does Esther's call for a three-day fast demonstrate her dependence on God? Why did she enlist the participation of others?

Did You Know?

Fasting acknowledges human frailty before God and appeals to His mercy. Fasting was a common practice in the ancient world, associated with mourning . . . intercessory prayer, . . . repentance and contrition for sin . . . and times of distress.

—*The Nelson Study Bible*

Consider the servants who kept Esther's confidences, carried messages to and from Mordecai, and fasted beside her. How did their presence demonstrate God's hand at work? How did their presence boost her courage?

Scan chapters 5 and 6 to discover more events that God was orchestrating. Summarize them, and comment on the fact that those most affected weren't aware of this supernatural intervention. When have you thought God was silent and distant, but later learned He had been working on your behalf?

Finally, read **Esther 7:1-4, 10**.

Comment on Esther's persuasive presentation to Xerxes. Pay attention to the tone, the climactic moment, and the outcome. How does this speech demonstrate that she'd been a good student of her culture? How does it demonstrate patient planning and self-control?

Where We Come In

God's name is never invoked in the book of Esther, but His presence is evident. Why is it important that this woman and this story be included in the Bible? What lessons about God do you learn from reading it?

Read the excerpt from *Staying True in a World of Lies*. How is Esther's situation similar to that of Daniel and his companions? How are her responses similar to theirs? (See Dan. 1:8–17.) What hope does this give you for the potential of today's young people to make good, God-centered choices?

Do you suppose Esther would have considered herself a role model? How is she a worthy role model to you today?

Whom do you trust? How did you come to trust them? Have they always been faithful? How have you proven that *you're* worthy of trust?

What character traits did Esther need to deal with her situation? Which of these do you need most to face your current challenges? What resources can you tap into for help?

Read the comments of university president Beverley Pitts. Then consider the topic of trust. Esther learned early that she had trustworthy people surrounding her. Beverley is careful whom she trusts. Which elements of Beverley's counsel apply most to your circumstances?

How It Works Today

Beverley Pitts is a university president and has mentored countless young women and scholars over her career as professor and administrator. As she mentors young women, she says:

"The value I bring to the institution is in . . . my judgment, my knowledge, my character, the way I interact with people. When you rise in a position and become a leader/manager, your character matters more and more. The effect of your character is greater because you can so easily ruin someone. So, of all the characteristics I care about, I care the most about the sense of respect and trust.

"Trust is about knowing you can count on consistency. What you see is what you get. It builds over time. It's not that I distrust people, but I have an ambiguous feeling about them when I first encounter them, and then I build trust. But once it's destroyed, it's just about lost forever.

"The most important thing to me is that people feel they can trust me. I feel an obligation to never let them down."

Consider trust from another angle: God's trustworthiness and faithfulness to His people. He placed Esther in the role of queen so He could save His people from annihilation. How has He worked similarly in your life? Is His trustworthiness to you dependent upon your trustworthiness to Him? Why or why not?

What Others Say

The king promoted an evil man and approved a wicked project. . . . The fact that God permits evil in this world does not mean that evil is good or that God is unconcerned or unable to help. When men do not allow Him to rule, He overrules, and He always accomplishes His purposes.

—Warren Wiersbe

Read the quote from Warren Wiersbe. When have you struggled to trust that God is good? What comfort do you find in knowing that though evil often seems to rule, God is always working to overrule the evil and accomplish His purposes? How does this answer some of your questions about why God allows evil temporary victories?

Responding through Prayer

Begin your prayer time by carrying to God a difficult situation that someone in your group is currently facing. Ask Him to intervene in the situation and to show you how He is already at work. Then listen silently for His response.

My Next Step

I identified the trait of _____ as the one I need most to face the challenges in my life. This week I will read and apply Scripture and seek wise counsel to build that trait in my character. I will begin by:

Keep It in Mind

For whatever courageous action you've determined to take, frequently repeat these comforting words: "Even though I walk through the valley of the shadow of death, I will fear no evil, for you [Lord] are with me" (Ps. 23:4).

6

Establishing A Lifestyle of Worship

Luke 2:22–38

There was also a prophetess, Anna, the daughter of Phanuel, of the tribe of Asher. She was very old; she had lived with her husband seven years after her marriage, and then was a widow until she was eighty-four. She never left the temple but worshiped night and day, fasting and praying.

—Luke 2:36–37

Discovery

Consistent worship is a courageous choice.

For Openers

It's Sunday morning, 5:26 a.m. A clock radio blares, interrupting my delicate snores. I grumble and punch my pillow. But at 5:30, I dutifully get up, make the bed, get showered, and make breakfast. On the way to church, I review my lesson—because I'm teaching Bible fellowship hour this week. We zigzag through traffic and succeed in beating a few choir members into the lot, securing for ourselves a better parking spot. We trudge through the slushy lot into the warm building—only to find the inner door locked. I leave my teaching materials and search for a janitor to let us in. Finally, in the classroom, I prepare the podium with my notes, hand off the PowerPoint presentation to Jerry (the computer guy), and say a quick prayer before socializing, singing, and finally teaching. After class, I climb the stairs to the sanctuary— hardly ready to enter God's holy presence in worship.

Your worship preparation is probably similar to mine. But today we'll meet a woman who can teach us plenty about worship. While she had every reason to be bitter with life, she parlayed her disappointments into opportunities to use her whole self in continuous worship.

Getting to Know Her

Luke summarizes Anna's story in three verses—but this scant scene culminates a life of courage. She is born late in the four-century period that we now call the "intertestamental" years. Much earlier, the people of Judah returned from captivity and repopulated the Promised Land. But for centuries since, the prophets of God have been strangely silent.

Anna's lifetime sees the subjection of Jerusalem to Roman rule in 63 B.C. and Herod the Great come to power around 40 B.C. Devout, orthodox worship of Jehovah is reestablished in the temple Herod builds and beautifies, and religious leaders exert great influence over the people—with sacrifices, festivals, and fasts, according to the covenant.

Anna marries like a typical young woman and lives with her husband for seven years, until his untimely death. She remains a widow well into old age. (Scripture is unclear as to whether she was widowed for eighty-four years or was eighty-four years old at the time of the story.)

Instead of wallowing in self-pity, Anna makes a courageous choice. She dedicates herself to constant devotion and service in God's Temple. She learns the promises God has made to His people. She prays. She fasts. She worships. And she waits for one key promise to be fulfilled at one miraculous moment.

Anna knows Simeon well, and she knows the promise the Holy Spirit made to him, that he won't die until he has seen the Deliverer. When she glances across the Temple courtyard and sees a curious glow on Simeon's face, she hurries to where he is—by this time holding a newborn child in his arms and speaking rapturous words of blessing. Her heart sings: *This is the One; the Deliverer has come! Blessed be the name of the Lord!* And she spreads the news among the faithful—*God's promise is being fulfilled, in our day, before our eyes!*

The Word Speaks

Choose three volunteers to read **Luke 2:22-38**. Have the first read the narration, the second read Simeon's words, and the third read Anna's words.

Discuss the deep honor and awe Anna has for God and how that affects her courageous choice to give up her old way of life and to reside in the Temple, as a server. Review some psalms Anna might have prayed during her years of prayer and fasting in the Temple. (Try Psalms 63, 65, 67, 111 and 116.)

Since Anna makes the Temple her home, she likely has heard the story of Zechariah's angel visitor and of his wife, Elizabeth, giving birth to John, prophesied to be the one to make straight the way of the Lord (Luke 1:76). How might this increase her anticipation? If you were Anna, what would you be thinking about the coming of the Messiah?

Bible Background

Anna the prophetess came from Asher, the tribe that was to be blessed and that was to "dip his foot in oil" (Deut. 33:24)—a sign of joy and happiness. But also, Asher's descendants were to have shoes of "iron and bronze," denoting strength (Deut. 33:25).

—Jack Hayford

Read the quote from Jack Hayford. How did Anna's early life measure up to the blessings promised to people of her tribe? How did her later life measure up? What choices made the difference?

As she was living through her husband's death—and experiencing the loneliness and poverty that followed—Anna couldn't have known what God had in store for her life. Comment on the reward God gave her. How did this climactic moment make all the sacrifice and all the sorrow worthwhile for her? How does this encourage you?

Read the quote from W. L. Walker. Now visualize the elder Simeon holding the infant Christ beside young Joseph; the elder prophetess Anna taking the arm of young Mary. Listen as Simeon speaks of the Child's promise and then gives the frightening prophesies—that He will cause the "falling and rising of many in Israel"; that He will be "a sign

> ## Did You Know?
>
> Old age was greatly desired and its attainment regarded as a Divine blessing (Gen. 15:15; Exod. 20:12) . . . Superior wisdom was believed to belong to the aged (Job 12:20; 15:10; 32:7, 9); hence positions of guidance and authority were given to them.
>
> —W. L. Walker

that will be spoken against"; that a sword will pierce Mary's soul. Why might God have allowed these two senior saints to bless, challenge, and enlighten the young parents? How is their age and experience a comfort—and a credible witness?

Where We Come In

What disappointments have come across your path? What circumstances have tempted you to become disillusioned or discouraged? How have you responded? How does Anna's choice to become a heart-deep worshiper challenge your responses and choices?

Which of your experiences with Christ might encourage someone else? Who would benefit from hearing your testimony of God's faithfulness?

Worship is not something we do as a luxury when we have the time in addition to other things we have to do. Worship is the very stuff of life, and while we are worshiping, God is working on our behalf and taking care of many things for us that we need to do.

—Anne Ortlund

Give your definition of *worship*. Then read the quote from Anne Ortlund. How does Anne's definition add layers of understanding? What does she mean when she says, "Worship is the very stuff of life"? If worship isn't limited to something we do corporately for an hour on Sunday mornings, what is it?

Read the quote from *The Message*, which summarizes Romans 12:1–2. The NIV calls this offering to God "your spiritual act of worship." How does this knowledge affect your understanding of worship? In what specific ways does it change your approach to everyday life?

Take your everyday, ordinary life—your sleeping, eating, going-to-work, and walking-around life—and place it before God as an offering. . . . Don't become so well-adjusted to your culture that you fit into it without even thinking. Instead, fix your attention on God. You'll be changed from the inside out.

—Romans 12:1–2, *The Message*

What things did you do or say last week that wouldn't fit this definition? How have you let culture seep in and adulterate your life's acts of worship to God? How can you prevent this from continuing to happen?

Read the story of Laura Edwards and Ruby Eliason. Discuss what these women gave up to offer God their lives as acts of worship. List the disappointments they endured along the way.

How It Works Today

Laura Edwards was a medical doctor with special training in obstetrics. She and her husband served a medical mission in India, where they opened a hospital for women and children. When the Indian government refused to renew their residence permit, they returned to the U.S., leaving behind a vibrant, growing group of Indian Christians.

Laura's colleague Ruby Eliason (Ph.D., health development) also evicted from India, spent the rest of her ministry in Cameroon, visiting isolated villages to help establish health standards, teach infant care, and make suggestions to improve public health.

After retirement, Ruby and then-widowed Laura spent fifteen winters back in Cameroon, in additional medical missions work. "I want to continue this important work," Laura said. Ruby added, "God has given me my health and preparation for continuing ministry, so why not do it?"

But on April 19, 2000, the Land Rover carrying the two women went off a mountainous road in a remote area of Cameroon. On that mountainside the two graduated from mission service into God's presence.

Why do you suppose they chose to continue on the mission field — giving themselves away for God's service — even through their retirement years? What heartfelt longings are evident in their comments? What do you make of the events of their death? How do their lives — and their deaths — challenge you to make sacrifices for Christ in your world? How do they challenge you not to hide behind excuses but to keep moving forward in God's work?

In what ways are they like the prophetess Anna? In what ways would you like to be more like all three of these godly women? What will you commit to do to take the next step in that direction?

Responding through Prayer

Allow each member of your group to speak a prayer of confession and dedication to God. You may use this prayer as a starter: *God, I haven't been living as though everything I do is an act of worship. Many of the things I've been doing aren't honoring to You at all. Forgive me, and grant me courage and strength to worship You in each moment.*

My Next Step

As I prepare my heart to enter corporate worship on Sunday, I will:

Keep It in Mind

Read Romans 12:1–2 in your favorite translation, and repeat it aloud daily. Recall your thoughts and deeds of the day, and honestly assess whether they align with the Scripture's call.

7

The Truth Confronts An Alien Culture

Acts 17:19–34

*Now what you worship as something unknown
I am going to proclaim to you.*

—Acts 17:23

Discovery

The courageous search for answers yields results.

For Openers

The publicity blitz for my book *Staying True in a World of Lies: Practical Models of Integrity for Women in the Workplace* took place as daily news reports focused on Martha Stewart's indictment for allegedly lying to federal authorities. Most reporters I did interviews with stuck with the scripted questions from my publicist, but one secular reporter had questions of her own. After a half hour of the regular questions, she finally blurted out, "If integrity will cost me something, why should I bother?"

Had the interview been with a Christian, I'd have answered that I do what's right because the Bible says so. Or that God would be displeased if I set out to do wrong. But she didn't have a God-centered worldview. So, I began with the worth of a good name, the importance of trustworthiness, and the freedom that comes from having a clear conscience when I place my head on my pillow at night — all valued, even in her world. Only after relating to her in this way could I explain my faith in Christ.

This may seem a roundabout approach, but it's not new. The Apostle Paul appealed to cultural relevance in the first century when addressing a group of Athenian thinkers. His speech convinced a few listeners to follow Christ, including the courageous female convert we'll meet today.

Getting to Know Her

The Athenian woman Damaris has spent years seeking knowledge. Foregoing the comforts of home and family that satisfy most of her contemporaries, she chooses a path of education that puts her in circles with the wisest men of her culture — not as wife or plaything, but as an invited conversant. She has heard every philosophy handed down from her ancient countrymen Plato and Socrates. Yet she seeks something more — something to satisfy her thirst for ultimate truth.

One day an odd-looking foreigner in rabbi's garments crosses her path. She eyes him — wandering the Acropolis, peering at statues of Athena, frowning as he weaves through temples and altars, appearing small amid the Parthenon's massive marble columns. She sees him pause at the altar dedicated "To the Unknown God." Then he begins to speak about a God she's never known. This man called Him the one true God; and although this concept is alien to her, it strangely draws her in.

When the men of the Areopagus council (where philosophical issues are debated) ask this rabbi to explain himself, she finds herself ascending the sixteen limestone steps to the top of Mars Hill, straining to hear his every word.

He speaks of God taking human form. Then he speaks of the Son of God dying for the people's sins. Incredibly, he concludes by claiming that this Son of God is resurrected from the dead—and remains alive forever. While the council members have only questions, this man has answers that seem to Damaris both utterly amazing and prospectively true. It will take a leap of faith, but if she dares to believe, this will mark the end of her lifelong search and the beginning of something far greater.

The Word Speaks

Recall anything you can about the architecture and culture of historic Greece. Envision yourself in that setting as someone reads aloud **Acts 17:19-34**. As the reader gets to Paul's speech to the Areopagus, imagine yourself in that crowd.

Did You Know?

The Greeks repudiated the idea of a bodily resurrection. Though they embraced the concept of the soul living forever, they were repulsed by the idea of a bodily resurrection because they considered the body to be evil, something to be discarded.

—The Nelson Study Bible

Read the note from *The Nelson Study Bible*. How does knowing this philosophy help you understand why Christ's resurrection became a stumbling block to the Athenians?

How did Paul integrate his observations about the city and his knowledge of their literature into his gospel presentation? Why do you think he did this?

Since Paul demonstrated a keen understanding of Greek culture—and a sensitivity to it in his opening statement—why did he consider Jesus' resurrection important enough to risk alienating his listeners? Why didn't he water down the message for the sake of cultural relevance? How are we tempted to water down the message of the Cross to make it more palatable for our peers? What is the danger in this?

What Others Say

Christianity is in its very essence a resurrection religion. The concept of resurrection lies at its heart. If you remove it, Christianity is destroyed.

—John R. W. Stott

Read the quotes from John Stott and Martin Luther. In your own words, explain how crucial the reality of Jesus' physical resurrection from the dead is to the Christian faith. How does Luther's claim (that resurrection is written in the fabric of the world we can see and touch) align with Paul's words in verses 24–27? How does the order and pattern of creation lead you to reach out for the Creator?

What Others Say

Our Lord has written the promise of the resurrection not in books alone, but in every leaf in springtime.

—Martin Luther

What do you suppose Damaris found appealing about Paul's argument? What part do you believe God's Holy Spirit played in drawing her to himself? (See John 14:26 and 1 Corinthians 2:14 for hints.)

Bible Background

Luke mentioned this woman among the Athenians who heard Paul speak and who responded to the gospel. Given the roles of women in Greek society, it is likely that she was a hetaera, a woman educated to be a companion of men rather than a wife. In Athens, wives were still secluded within the home.

—S. P. and L. Richards

Read the quote from S. P. and L. Richards. Damaris had spent her lifetime being inculcated with the philosophies of her day, so what kind of courage do you think it took for a woman of this training to come to faith in Christ? How might the mocking of her contemporaries challenge her fledgling faith? Comment on the significance of Luke, the author of the book of Acts, mentioning Damaris by name, while identifying some converts simply as "a number of others."

Where We Come In

How much of your commitment to Christ is based on information
that you can prove to be true? How much is based on faith—taking God at His Word, despite a lack of tangible evidence to back
it up? Consider your answer in light of Hebrews 11:1, 6.

Which elements of Christ's story are the hardest for you to believe
or comprehend? Which elements are the biggest stumbling blocks
to postmodern thinkers?

When a reporter asked best-selling author Jerry Jenkins how he
could justify his claim that Jesus is the only way to God, Jerry
quoted Jesus' words, "I am the way and the truth and the life. No one
comes to the Father except through me" (John 14:6). He continued,
"That's not my idea; that's what He said . . . and I believe it to be
true." How would you have answered? Discuss whether a postmodern thinker would find this answer satisfying. If the reporter was not
satisfied with the answer, what might you have said next?

Read the story of Ethel Herr. Paying special attention to how she grew
her faith—by getting alone with God to read His Word and pray—discuss with the group where you've searched for answers to your questions of faith. What circumstances prompted these questions? (For
example, did they come out of times of crisis, like Ethel experienced
when her father abandoned the family? Or did they come out of times
of plenty, when having all you'd ever wanted wasn't enough?)

How It Works Today

This is the story of Christian author and prayer warrior Ethel Herr:

"My preacher-father ran off with one of the teenagers in our congregation and moved Mother, my brother, and me to California to begin a new life without him. We literally lived from one meal to another. But we spent a lot of time on our knees. All we needed, God provided. My mother refused to be bitter.

"Often on a summer day, we would escape our hot home and go to a local park. My favorite thing to do on those occasions was to sneak off by myself with my Bible, and just read and pray. One of the greatest things I learned, which impacted my prayer life profoundly, was that earthly fathers are flawed and always will be. But I have a heavenly Father who is totally without flaws. He will always take care of me, so I can go to Him in absolute confidence with anything I need to share with someone. And, while I know He'll not always give me what I ask—because that's not what is best—He will listen and give me what He knows to be best."

Ask the group to wrestle with each question you've encountered—either in your search for Christ, or as you've engaged others in conversations about Him. Try to find support from the Bible to help you come up with viable answers.

If a reporter were to ask you to give the reason you choose to live God's way, how would you respond? What if you were asked by a colleague? A classmate? A boss? A judge? What risks would you be taking to answer fully and truthfully?

In what ways could you use current events and popular culture to engage someone's interest in the things of God? How would you transition from those events into the subject of faith?

Responding through Prayer

Make this your heart's prayer: *God, I am grateful that You made yourself known and knowable, not just in the natural world, but in Your Son Jesus. Thank You for providing my way into Your presence through Him. Let me not be content following You by myself. Give me words and opportunities to lead others into relationship with You, just as Paul led Damaris.*

My Next Step

This week I will:

- Pay special attention to the topics of conversation among unbelievers; I will pray for the wisdom to present God's good news to them in a way that is both completely true and completely relevant to real-life issues.

-

Keep It in Mind

Each day this week, meditate on the profound truth of this familiar verse: *"That if you confess with your mouth, 'Jesus is Lord,' and believe in your heart that God raised him from the dead, you will be saved"* (Rom. 10:9).

8

A Sensitive Teacher Receives Her Reward

Acts 18:1–3, 18–28

*Greet Priscilla and Aquila, my fellow workers in Christ Jesus.
They risked their lives for me. Not only I but all the
churches of the Gentiles are grateful to them.*

—Romans 16:3–4

Discovery

The courage to follow God brings true fulfillment.

For Openers

My first geometry teacher drilled into my head the rule (or was it a postulate?) that the shortest distance between two points is a straight line. It's a concept so ingrained in my psyche that whenever I slide into the driver's seat of my Mitsubishi, I sift through my mental database to choose the most direct route between where I am and where I'm going.

But when I'm driving a long distance, a MapQuest search often selects a longer route, so I can travel an interstate rather than surface streets. Often the interstate takes me on a loopy path, curving around obstacles, bypassing cities, and occasionally going north to end up south.

Does this seem as odd to you as it does to me? But what's so great about choosing the shortest distance anyway? A straight path through life would be mind-numbing, adventure-less, and tedious. The circuitous route God usually chooses for our lives takes us in directions we'd never have envisioned, and affords opportunities we'd never have thought possible. Such is the case with today's woman, the New Testament traveling gal Priscilla. Her route was convoluted—but God always had her in the right place at the right time.

Getting to Know Her

We can piece together the story of Priscilla from several New Testament passages. First, she is living with her husband, Aquila, in Rome. But in A.D. 49 Claudius evicts Jews from the capital. The two pack up their tentmaking business and move to the port city of Corinth, fifty miles from Athens.

As they settle in the Jewish guild and synagogue, another Jewish tentmaker, Paul, is on his way from Athens to Corinth. The three meet and establish a business partnership as well as a partnership in eternal matters. The couple may have come to faith in Christ prior to meeting Paul (according to Acts 2:9, some Jews from Aquila's home city, Pontus, were converted at Pentecost), but as they work with Paul and as he lives in their home, they grow in knowledge of Jesus Christ.

After many months, the apostle sails on to Ephesus; Priscilla and Aquila sail with him. At some point, the couple seize the opportunity to save Paul's life; however, specific circumstances aren't recorded for posterity.

Paul leaves them in Ephesus as he continues his journey. There they shepherd the fledgling church and meet the young evangelist Apollos, who knows only of the baptism of John. Patiently and privately, Priscilla and Aquila invite this man into their home and disciple him in the full gospel. They do such a thorough job that Apollos is equipped to refute detractors publicly and serve the church well in coming years.

From Ephesus, the husband and wife move back to Rome, where they host a church in their home. They keep tabs on Paul—and he on them—as their ministry partnership continues across the miles and across the years.

The Word Speaks

Silently read **Acts 18:1-3, 18-28**.

Underline each mention of Priscilla and the active role she took in tentmaking and the faith development of herself and others. Share what you observe.

Other passages also mention Priscilla and Aquila. Look up Romans 16:3–5; 1 Corinthians 16:19; and 2 Timothy 4:19. What do these verses add to your understanding of Priscilla's sacrifice for the gospel? What opposition did she encounter as she served Christ alongside her husband and Paul? What key character traits did she demonstrate?

Corinth was a hotbed of temple prostitution and immorality; Ephesus was the center of worship for the Greek goddess Artemis (the city's temple to her was one of the Seven Wonders of the Ancient World). How might godly Priscilla have felt about relocating to such heathen locales?

What were some reasons God allowed Priscilla and Aquila to be evicted from Rome? After they experienced such joy in establishing a long-time friendship with Paul, how do you suppose the couple felt when he moved on to more adventures but left them behind in Ephesus? What role was God calling them to serve in Ephesus?

How was Priscilla's sweet spirit and sensitivity in teaching Apollos in private (rather than embarrassing him in public) evident in his response—and the ultimate result?

Read the note about first-century house churches. Imagine yourself as a church member in Rome, receiving a letter from the renowned Apostle Paul (whom you've never met). How would you have felt as you heard his epistle to the Romans read aloud—specifically verses 16:3–5? How does this reassure you, even today, that you are part of something great—something that transcends time and space—as a member of the church?

Bible Background

Early Christians built no large churches or cathedrals. Instead they met in homes for worship and sharing. Based on the size of homes in first-century cities, meetings must have accommodated a very limited number of people. Yet as Paul's letters show, there was a sense of identity with the greater body of all believers who lived in the city, and beyond that with believers throughout the world.

—*Bible Reader's Companion*

Where We Come In

If you have ever been called to move to a new location for the sake of work or ministry, share your feelings about that move with the group. How did you see God's hand at work in the process?

What did you have to leave behind? Who were some of the people you missed most? What adventures did God have in store for you that you'd never have encountered if you'd stayed behind?

After reading the quote from John Newton (better known as lyricist of the hymn "Amazing Grace") identify disappointments or redirections from God that you have experienced. How do the words of Newton and Roberts comfort you? How do they challenge you?

What Others Say

I can hardly recollect a single plan of mine . . . that, had it taken place in season and circumstance just as I proposed, it would, humanly speaking, have . . . deprived me of the greater good the Lord had designed for me.

—John Newton

Out of every disappointment there is treasure. Satan whispers, 'All is lost.' God says, 'Much can be gained.

—Frances J. Roberts

Reading Priscilla's story, you can't help but recognize her love for the church. What can you do to nurture your love for the church? What gifts has God given you that would be beneficial to your local church?

Read the quote from S. P. and L. Richards. Think in terms of your marriage, or a modern-day marriage you've observed. How typical is this model of a marriage partnership? What role do you suppose this partnership plays in freeing both Priscilla and Aquila to accomplish God's purposes for them? How could you apply

Did You Know?

That Priscilla is named first in three passages and Aquila is also named first in three indicates that these two truly were equal partners. . . . They were partners in life and in ministry.

—S. P. and L. Richards

observations about their marriage to your closest family relationships? What difference might changing your perspective make?

Read the story of Phoenix politician Peggy Bilsten. Comment on the winding path God used to bring her to a place of influence. Pay special attention to His perfect timing all along the way. What gifts and opportunities did God give to her? What passions did He place in her heart? How is she using those talents in her public life and in her faith community? Which elements of Peggy's example give you ideas about how you could use your influence to accomplish great things for Christ?

How It Works Today

Twenty years ago, Peggy Bilsten was a wife, mom of two tots, and kindergarten teacher. Nine years later, she was elected to serve as a Phoenix councilwoman. Before and since, Peggy has taken her faith to work. She participates in a Bible study called "Employees for Christ," which has a prayer group in every city facility and hosts an Internet site that allows anyone to share prayer requests. She is known state-wide as an advocate for victims of domestic violence.

During a term as Phoenix's vice mayor, she was reading in Matthew about Jesus washing the disciples' feet. So, when she heard of a need on the other side of the world, she responded, "Jesus would have been there with these people." She recommended that the city partner with Phoenix-based ministry Food for the Hungry to adopt a sister city and provide humanitarian aid. Twice, Peggy has visited the sister city—first to discern the need, then to deliver $200,000 in aid collected by Phoenix residents. Part of this aid provided pedal taxis so the most poverty-stricken people could have the means to create a permanent income. Not bad for a kindergarten teacher who made herself available to God's meandering plan.

Responding through Prayer

Take a few moments to reflect on the path God has chosen for you. Thank Him for His consistent presence. Ask for continued guidance and direction as you make decisions this week. Pray that you'll make the most of every opportunity to serve Him—no matter where He takes you.

My Next Step

Without fanfare and without seeking glory for myself, I will show how much I love Christ's church this week by serving my local body of believers in the following ways:

Keep It in Mind

If you'll commit to using your talents for God's glory, you'll receive this amazing reward: "God . . . will not forget your work and the love you have shown him as you have helped his people and continue to help them" (Heb. 6:10).